Heaven Made You

Heaven
Made You

Kimberly Hazlett,
Illustrated by Mandy Adendorff

NEW YORK

NASHVILLE • MELBOURNE • VANCOUVER

Heaven Made You

Published in New York, New York, by Morgan James Publishing. Morgan James is a trademark of Morgan James, LLC. www.MorganJamesPublishing.com

The Morgan James Speakers Group can bring authors to your live event. For more information or to book an event visit The Morgan James Speakers Group at www.TheMorganJamesSpeakersGroup.com.

ISBN 978-1-68350-963-9 paperback
ISBN 978-1-68350-964-6 eBook
Library of Congress Control Number: 2018933362

Cover Design by:
Rachel Lopez
www.r2cdesign.com

Interior Design by:
Bonnie Bushman
The Whole Caboodle Graphic Design

In an effort to support local communities, raise awareness and funds, Morgan James Publishing donates a percentage of all book sales for the life of each book to Habitat for Humanity Peninsula and Greater Williamsburg.

Get involved today! Visit www.MorganJamesBuilds.com.

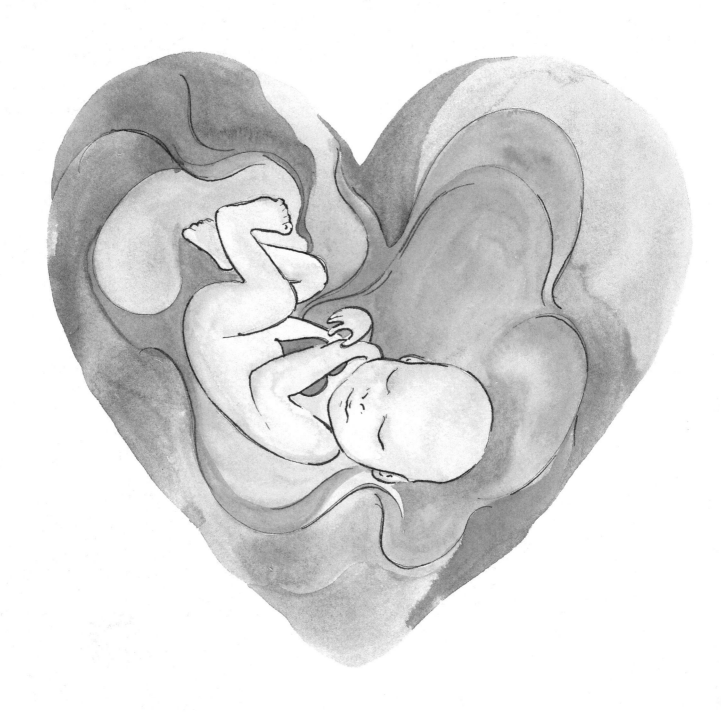

Tiny fingers

little nose

all the way down

to your delicate toes

You were formed

in the heart

of a very big God

You were formed in the

of a very

BiG
GOD

Inside out, all of your ways were known by your Maker before you lived one of your days

Eyes of wonder,
ears to hear,
hands to praise
your Father so near

You were formed in the ♥ of a very kind God

Y ou were formed

in the heart of

a very kind God

A bright mind to learn,

a heart that is true,

Gifts deep inside

all from the

Father to you

Heaven made you
Held out the plan
to save you

Set you apart

Gave you a heart
like your Maker

The Father sang your song,
the angels danced along

When Heaven Made You

About the Author

Kimberly Hazlett is a Singer/Songwriter and Piano teacher with a keen desire to encourage each of her students to grow in their God-given gifts and creativity. Kimberly holds a degree in Religious Education and has taught in classrooms from Kindergarten to third grade. Her popular lullaby CD, "Heaven Made You," is the inspiration behind the book and thousands of copies of the CD have delighted young children across the country and overseas. Originally from Pennsylvania, Kimberly has lived in Massachusetts, New Hampshire and currently resides in Connecticut with her husband and two grown daughters.

About the Illustrator

Mandy Adendorff is an award-winning artist, international speaker, and published author. Her originals and print collections adorn residences and corporations in the USA and abroad. Mandy studied art at the National School of the Arts in Johannesburg, South Africa. She was also born in Johannesburg, South Africa and currently resides in Simsbury, Connecticut.

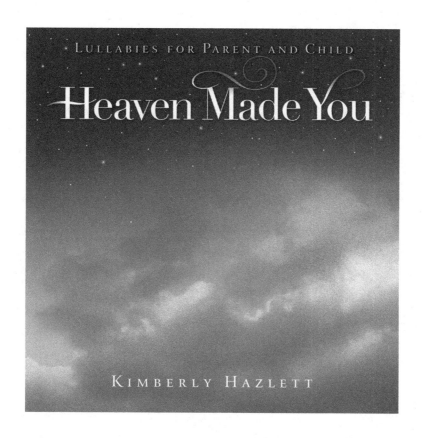

A collection of songs for instilling security in the night-time hours. Children and parents alike will take comfort while listening to beautiful melodies and lyrics that affirm our place of origin as Heaven in the heart of a loving God.

Here is where you can purchase the CD:
http://bobhazlett.org/product/heaven-made-you-cd/

9 781683 509639